and nits. We weren't dirty; even the poshest Glasgow children would have had their hair nit-combed weekly sixty years ago.

Clothes were patched and darned until the patches and darns joined together, and what could be passed on from one child to another was passed on, and on, and on. Things were passed down in families and between neighbours too. Of course there were fall-outs, but neighbours were real neighbours, in good times and in bad. Fall-outs were short, sharp and mostly soon forgotten.

We were poor; we were all poor. In fact, our part of Paisley was one of the poorest places in Europe when I was growing up. But we didn't know we were poor and we were no worse than anyone else in the street, and were better off than some.

MY OWN FREE WILL

When I was fifteen years old, I chose of my own free will to go down the wrong road. When a girl I knew asked if I wanted to chip in for a half bottle of wine, I happily handed over the money. Then I went up a close (an alley) and took my first mouthful of the stuff, and discovered confidence for the first time.

I was still fifteen when I was taken to hospital in a drunken and drugged coma, and I was there for months. In a way, hospital suited me. I didn't need to think. We had no choices to make. Clothes appeared and we put them on. Food arrived on the table and we ate it. We sat most of the day, stoned out of our minds with the drugs we were given. I went from being stoned with drink and illegal drugs to be stoned with what was brought to me by nurses. And being stoned suited me; it stopped me feeling. When I eventually got out of hospital, the

PRECIOUS
TO GOD

May Nicholson

PRECIOUS TO GOD

When I was a girl growing up in Ferguslie Park in Paisley in the 1950s, everyone was poor, but we lived in a real community. If there was a problem, the women sat and talked about it, sharing their cares and their worries. Sometimes, they just sat on their doorsteps, still wearing their aprons and talked and talked. Maybe they looked as though they were wasting their time, but they weren't. Apart from anything else, they needed to sit down for a rest. Bringing up a family was hard work. Women did the washing bent over scrubbing boards, rubbing the clothes up and down the hard ridges until their shoulders ached and their hands were sore.

Hair-washing was a weekly event, usually done on Fridays, and normally followed by the dreaded nit-comb. We sat down on a hard chair with a newspaper underneath it, and our hair was tugged through a fine metal comb to get rid of any lice

first thing I thought of was getting another drink. Drink took away my self respect and even my sanity – I mean that – and it could easily have taken my life. There are people I used to drink with who didn't survive their addiction.

My wee mother used to break her heart. 'Is it me? Is it me?' she asked, over and over and over again. We'd been poor right enough, but she'd brought up my older brothers and sisters without them going off the rails and breaking her heart. cried too and asked, 'Why am I like this? There was no answe for Mum. And the only answer for me was that I was a drunk and a junkie because that's what I'd chosen to be.

Eventually, my family met and at first the idea was to send me to America, but I persuaded them to let me go to Jersey instead. I had a cousin there and I thought that he and could live it up together. So, with Mum's money in my pocket, I se out for my new life.

IN THE PITS

There's a story in the Bible that was my story. Jesus spoke about a prodigal son who persuaded his father to give him his share of the family money and he went off and spent it all. As long as he had money he had plenty of friends, but when his money ran out they were nowhere to be seen. He had to go down to the pits – looking after a herd of pigs and eating pigswill because he was so hungry – before he came to his senses. And when he did, he went right home to his father, who threw a party because his son had come back. I was like that prodigal. I took my mum's money, and she must have scrimped and saved to give it to me, and headed off for the bright lights of Jersey.

My cousin and I had a great time … until one day the Police were looking for us. We had stolen and crashed a car. I wasn't sober enough to remember how it had happened.

THE BRIGHT LIGHTS

The next thing I knew I was in Blackpool, penniless and on the streets. After a couple of nights sleeping rough, I contacted my mum and asked her to wire money to a Post Office in Blackpool to get me home.

Although she hated what I was doing to myself, Mum loved me. She wired enough for my bus fare and, when I arrived home, there was a big pan of stovies on the cooker and the water was heated for a bath.

God loves sinners, although he hates their sin. God is so holy that He can't even look on sin. So there's no way any single one of us could go to heaven to be with Him, for we are all miserable sinners whether we know it or not, whether we are drunks and drug addicts or 'respectable'. Sin needs to be punished, and the amazing thing is that Jesus, God's Son, willingly accepted our punishment on the cross so that those who believe in him should be washed clean and taken home to heaven when they die. God loves sinners so much that he gave his Son Jesus to die on the cross so that our sin could be taken away from us forever. My brain can't begin to take that in, but God's Word says it, so it's true. God doesn't tell lies.

FLOODS OF TEARS

To cut a long story short, I married and had a daughter, Tracey. You would have thought that having a lovely wee daughter would have stopped me drinking. It didn't. Mum and the rest of my family came to Tracey's rescue many a time when I was drunk and incapable.

When Tracey was ten, her little brother was born. Although I'd spent a lot of my pregnancy in a psychiatric hospital, God gave us a lovely, healthy, baby boy. Before we left the maternity unit I promised Alan that he'd have a very different start to life from his big sister. He didn't. He was a toddler when I sobered up enough one morning to realise that Alan was wandering around the house in yesterday's clothes and still wearing yesterday's nappy. That hit me like a ton of bricks. Apart from my family, there was only one other person who would ever let me into her house. I changed and dressed Alan and then went to see her.

It turned out that she was going to a meeting that night and I said I'd go with her, though I'd no idea where she was going. It could have been a bingo club, for all I knew. She tried to put me off, telling me I was filthy (true), disgusting (true), and that my clothes were a mess (all of this was true) and that I wasn't going with her. If she'd asked me to go, I'd probably have backed out of it, but her attitude made me determined. I followed her to the meeting, which turned out to be a collection of former alcoholics who were trying to keep off the drink with God's help.

When I followed my friend in, I found a group of people sitting in a circle, singing! Then they read a bit from a book. I didn't know it was the Bible. After that, there was a prayer, and by the time one of the men prayed for me I was in floods of tears. I didn't think I was worth a prayer. I still remember the words

8

of his prayer; they burnt into my heart. He prayed, 'Lord, I pray for that woman you've brought here tonight. We can all see that she's filthy by looking at the outside of her, but you know how much more filthy her heart is. Touch her and clean her.' God answered that prayer, and I left the meeting a forgiven sinner.

GOD DID IT ALL

As soon as I became a Christian, I had a great love for people who didn't know Jesus. I was worried that they were going to hell. I was a missionary from day one. I used to go round the streets telling whoever would listen that Jesus was my Saviour and he was willing to be their Saviour too.

The day after I was converted, I cleaned the house from top to bottom. It had been filthy. When I was tidying a cupboard I found half a bottle of whisky. I poured it all down the sink. The only alcohol I've drunk since then is sips of Communion wine. My house was clean, my children had a mother, and I was sober day and night. I could never have done any of that myself. God did it all, every single bit of it.

One evening, when I was chatting with some Christian friends, we asked each other what we wanted to do with our lives. It had been decades since I'd even thought about such a thing,

but I knew the answer. When my turn came I heard myself saying, 'I'd like to have millions and millions of Jesus' love so that wherever I go it will spill out on the people I meet who are unwanted, not needed and unloved.'

My neighbours were amazed at the total change. They watched for me coming up the street drunk, and at night they listened for the police car taking me home drunk and incapable. But instead of cursing and swearing at them I stopped and talked to them about Jesus. Some asked me what had changed and I wasn't slow to tell them! A number of my neighbours were thrilled. I suppose they were also relieved because it couldn't have been nice living near me. Others raised their eyebrows when I told them about my conversion. I could see they thought that drink and drugs had made me lose my senses completely. The truth was that I was talking sense for the very first time. Even several taxi drivers, who knew me well from picking me off the pavement outside pubs and taking me home, stopped and asked what had happened.

I'VE GOT THE ANSWER

There was one man I desperately wanted to talk to, the psychiatrist who had looked after me for years. I phoned the hospital and asked to speak to him. He probably thought he was going to get a drunken tirade.

'Dr S,' I said, 'I've got the answer to a lot of your patients' problems.'

By then he was no doubt sure I was drunk, but he waited patiently to hear what I had to say.

'When I was in your hospital, I was doped to the eyeballs and sat around for weeks like a zombie,' I told him. 'And in that state you can forget your past and all your shame and guilt. But when the drugs wear off, the shame and guilt are still there. Drugs don't take them away.' I was so excited as I went on with my good news. 'Dr S, Jesus Christ has taken away all

my guilt and shame. It's as though he took it from me and put it in a river beside a sign that says "No fishing". I can't fish my past up now and neither can anyone else.'

That was when Dr S realised that I was stone-cold-sober. I don't think he could believe what he was hearing. I've met him and some of the nurses from that hospital since then. 'You're a miracle,' one of them told me. I agreed, and explained that I was a miracle of God's grace.

Probably nobody was happier at what had happened than Mum. I explained that I'd become a Christian and that I had to make amends for all the hurts I'd caused her.

'You don't need to make amends at all,' she told me. 'The amends are made because I can go to bed and sleep at nights without listening for the police coming up the stairs to tell me that you are in prison, or the hospital phoning to say you're having your stomach pumped.'

To show how much she trusted the new me, Mum gave me a key to the house. I'd not had a key since I'd stolen the house key when I was fourteen years old.

Some years later, when Mum was dying, she said to my auntie, 'I can go away and be with my Maker now, for I know that May is all right.' Those were her last words. And she did go to be with her Maker because Mum also became a Christian. That was one of the most wonderful ways that God restored the years that I'd wasted on drink and drugs. He gave me back to Mum and he gave Mum back to me for us to love and appreciate each other.

MAKING AMENDS

God showed me that there were places where I had to make amends. When I was drinking I once stole money from a collection box in a church and I went back to repay it. The old minister had gone away and a new one was there. I gave him £5 and explained that it was for repayment and amends. 'I can't accept this,' he told me, kindly. When I insisted and explained that God had shown me that was what I had to do, he took the money. Over the years, I've seen just the same thing happen with new Christians. The Lord has shown them too that they have to make reparation for what they have stolen or damaged.

At the same time, I became very involved in working with people who suffered from drug and alcohol addictions. I wanted to help however I could. Soon I was giving my testimony at meetings. The first time I was asked to tell how I became a Christian, I was petrified! I got up to speak and halfway through, I dried up. Not a word would come. Then, I said that

none of my family would believe that May Nicholson was lost for words! The people at the meeting laughed and that gave me a minute to think. I was just amazed at what God had done. A few months earlier, I'd been a no-hoper, drowning my sorrows in drink and drugs, using every way I could think of to escape from myself. Now, I was standing up in front of groups of people, telling them that Jesus had forgiven me for all that, and that he'd released me from my addictions. God was very good to me because he took me off drink and drugs without any of the terrible withdrawals that many people go through. I don't know why he did that. It's not the same for everyone who is trying to come off. Another thing that amazed me was that God used my testimony to help people from all sorts of backgrounds, poor folk like me and wealthy professional people too, people who wouldn't have looked at the ground I stood on before I was converted. Over those months, I saw wonderful things happening in some folk's lives.

ANOTHER BEGINNING

God spoke to me after I'd been a Christian for about six or seven months. I don't mean that I heard a voice speaking in my ears, but I heard him in my heart, just as clearly as I heard people actually speaking to me. He asked me why I didn't do the work I was doing through the church. I approached the minister and asked if this was a possibility. 'You'd have to give up your job to join the team,' Ian Maxwell, the associate minister, pointed out. I thought about the money I earned as a linen maid and hesitated. Ian realised that we really did need that money and offered to help find support for me. Before long, financial support came from across the United Kingdom!

This was the beginning of my life working for the church and Glasgow City Mission and then stepping out in faith to start

Preshal, a ministry that works with families, caring for them, valuing them and providing spiritual and practical care. To put it another way, we try to show folk that they are precious to us and even more precious to God.

If anyone had told me, before I was converted, how my life would turn out, I would have laughed until I couldn't laugh any more. I was a no-hoper; my life was worth nothing. The truth is that if I hadn't stopped drinking I would have died long ago. When I look back at old photos I can see that I look younger now than I did when I was twenty-five years old.

If I'd known God's plans, I would never have believed they were possible. But God is great. The Bible says, '"For I know the plans I have for you," declares the Lord, "plans to prosper you and not to harm you, plans to give you a hope and a future. Then you will call on me and come and pray to me, and I will listen to you. You will seek me and find me when you seek me with all your heart"' (Jeremiah 29:11-13).

For someone who had never fitted in anywhere (at least, not when I was sober) I was totally blown away by the feeling of being part of the Christian church. It was my family. God's plans have taken me along some very strange roads, but I've gone along them in his company and in the company of his precious people.

LUKE 15:11-32 - THE PRODIGAL SON

¹¹ And he said, "There was a man who had two sons. ¹² And the younger of them said to his father, 'Father, give me the share of property that is coming to me.' And he divided his property between them. ¹³ Not many days later, the younger son gathered all he had and took a journey into a far country, and there he squandered his property in reckless living. ¹⁴ And when he had spent everything, a severe famine arose in that country, and he began to be in need. ¹⁵ So he went and hired himself out to one of the citizens of that country, who sent him into his fields to feed pigs. ¹⁶ And he was longing to be fed with the pods that the pigs ate, and no one gave him anything.

¹⁷ "But when he came to himself, he said, 'How many of my father's hired servants have more than enough bread, but I perish here with hunger! ¹⁸ I will arise and go to my father, and I will say to him, "Father, I have sinned against heaven and before you. ¹⁹ I am no longer worthy to be called your son. Treat me as one of your hired servants."' ²⁰ And he arose and came to his father. But while he was still a long way off, his father saw him and felt compassion, and ran and embraced him and kissed him. ²¹ And the son said to him, 'Father, I have sinned against heaven and before you. I am no longer worthy to be called your son.' ²² But the father said to his servants, 'Bring quickly the best robe, and put it on him, and put a ring on his hand, and shoes on his feet. ²³ And bring the fattened calf and kill it, and let us eat and celebrate. ²⁴ For this my son was dead, and is alive again; he was lost, and is found.' And they began to celebrate.

²⁵ "Now his older son was in the field, and as he came and drew near to the house, he heard music and dancing.

²⁶ And he called one of the servants and asked what these things meant. ²⁷ And he said to him, 'Your brother has come, and your father has killed the fattened calf, because he has received him back safe and sound.' ²⁸ But he was angry and refused to go in. His father came out and entreated him, ²⁹ but he answered his father, 'Look, these many years I have served you, and I never disobeyed your command, yet you never gave me a young goat, that I might celebrate with my friends. ³⁰ But when this son of yours came, who has devoured your property with prostitutes, you killed the fattened calf for him!' ³¹ And he said to him, 'Son, you are always with me, and all that is mine is yours. ³² It was fitting to celebrate and be glad, for this your brother was dead, and is alive; he was lost, and is found.'"

A MESSAGE FROM MAY

My story is very like the parable of the prodigal son in the Bible. He took his father's money and went to a land far away. He spent his money on drink, drugs and partying. You name it, he did it. You name it, I did it! I ended up on the streets, dirty, filthy and eating from bins.

The prodigal son ended up feeding pigs and wanting to eat their food. But when he got back, his father ran to meet him, he put a cloak on his back and shoes on his feet and a ring on his finger and they had one big party. When I got back home, my mother had run a hot bath and cooked me a good meal.

What do these stories tell me? The first one tells me about my mother and how she hated the sin, but boy, how much she loved the sinner! The parable of the prodigal son tells me of Father God. No matter what we do, where we go, where we end up, he is always waiting with his arms open wide to welcome us back.

I have one son and I would never give up his life for anyone or anything. Yet, we have a Father God in Heaven who loves us so much that he sent his Son to die on a cross for sinners like us. Is this not a wonderful love that God has for us? He sent the very best that heaven has, to die for the very worst.

Pray to God now. Ask him to receive you as his child. His word says: "For God so loved the world that he gave his one and only Son, that whoever believes in him shall not perish but have eternal life." John 3:16

May Nicholson with Sir Alex Ferguson, former manager of Manchester United and patron of The Preshal Trust.

THE PRESHAL TRUST

Preshal is the Gaelic for "precious" – and that is how we feel about everyone who comes through our doors. We are a recognised Christian charity. In a friendly, caring, loving and supportive way Preshal seeks to tackle, head-on, the problem of social exclusion in the Linthouse area of Glasgow. This problem is manifested in poverty, alcohol and drug addiction, low literacy and numeracy levels, depression and low self-esteem. The Trust, working with other agencies, provides a wide range of social, recreational and educational activities which enable these issues to be dealt with effectively. We adopt an holistic approach whereby we seek to cater for the whole person, including meeting individual physical, mental and – as a Christian rooted organisation - spiritual needs.

The Preshal Trust, PO Box 7344, 8 Aboukir Street, Glasgow, G51 4QX
email: preshaltrust@hotmail.com

BLYTHSWOOD CARE

Blythswood Care provides practical help, love and support for those in need. Whether through filled shoeboxes at Christmas, relief and development aid or social projects for young and old, Blythswood brings hope to families in Europe, Africa and Asia. For every £1 donated, Blythswood delivers more than £5 worth of grass roots aid. With the support of ordinary people like you, Blythswood achieves EXTRAORDINARY transformations and provides loving care for body and soul.

Head Office: Highland Deephaven, Evanton, Ross-shire, Scotland, IV16 9XJ   email: info@blythswood.org

Photographs
Page 2: By Magnus Hagdorn from UK (Meadow Lane Graffiti) [CC BY-SA 2.0
(http://creativecommons.org/licenses/by-sa/2.0)], via Wikimedia Commons
Page 12: By Waldemarpaetz Troutster.com (Own work) [CC BY 3.0 (http://
creativecommons.org/licenses/by/3.0)], via Wikimedia Commons
Page 18: By D. Sharon Pruitt from Hill Air Force Base, Utah, USA [CC BY 2.0
(http://creativecommons.org/licenses/by/2.0)], via Wikimedia Commons

Copyright © May Nicholson 2015
10 9 8 7 6 5 4 3 2 1
ISBN: 978-1-7-8191-651-3
Published in 2015
by
Christian Focus Publications, Geanies House,
Fearn, Ross-shire, IV20 1TW, Scotland, U.K.
www.christianfocus.com
Cover design by Daniel van Straaten
Printed and bound in China

Christian Focus Publications

Christian Focus Christian CF4K Mentor
Focus Heritage

CHRISTIAN FOCUS PUBLICATIONS

Christian Focus Publications publishes books for adults and children under its four main imprints: Christian Focus, CF4K, Mentor and Christian Heritage. Our books reflect our conviction that God's Word is reliable and Jesus is the way to know him, and live for ever with him.

Our children's publication list includes a Sunday School curriculum that covers pre-school to early teens, and puzzle and activity books. We also publish personal and family devotional titles, biographies and inspirational stories that children will love.

If you are looking for quality Bible teaching for children then we have an excellent range of Bible stories and age-specific theological books. From pre-school board books to teenage apologetics, we have it covered!

Christian Focus Publications
Geanies House
Fearn, Tain, Ross-shire
IV20 1TW
Scotland, U.K.
email: info@christianfocus.com

At fifteen years of age, May Nicholson was an alcoholic and had even suffered an overdose-induced coma. In her local town of Paisley, Scotland, she became a notorious fighting drunkard.

But May's story is one of transformation through God's extravagant love! It will move you to tears, to laughter and to prayer. God brought her through terrible times to find faith and hope.

Read May's story and you will discover that – whatever your circumstances, whatever your needs, whatever your addictions – you too are precious to God!

May Nicholson is the founder of the Preshal Trust, a charity set up to tackle social exclusion in Glasgow. May was an alcoholic but found hope and freedom through Jesus.

The Preshal Trust

CHRISTIAN
FOCUS
Good Books with the
Real Message of Hope

CHRISTIAN FOCUS
PUBLICATIONS

www.preshaltrust.org.uk   www.christianfocus.com

ISBN 978-1-78191-651-3

9 781781 916513

Biography, BIC – HRC/YTH/BIO
Read to me: 12, Read myself: 12-16